KALI'S STORY
An Orphaned Polar Bear Rescue

By Jennifer Keats Curtis
Photography by John Gomes

P9-DNW-082

"GGRRR," growled the small, fluffy, white bear as the man pulled him out of the icy den.

"Please don't bite me, little one," whispered the man, "I'm only trying to help. Your momma just died. Without her, you won't last long out here by yourself. I have to get you some help."

With that, the man revved up his snowmobile and raced the baby polar bear to his village for help.

The villagers tried to feed the polar bear cub some milk. But like human newborns, the baby bear drank from his mother, not a bowl or a cup.

They named the cub Kali (pronounced Cully) after their village.

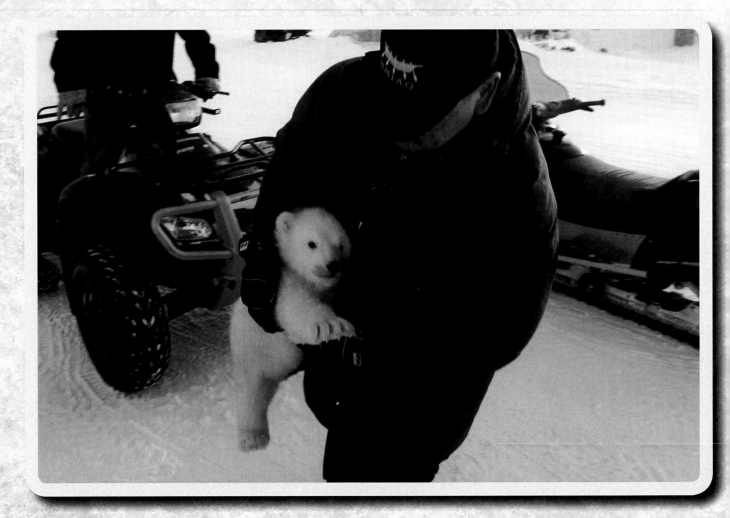

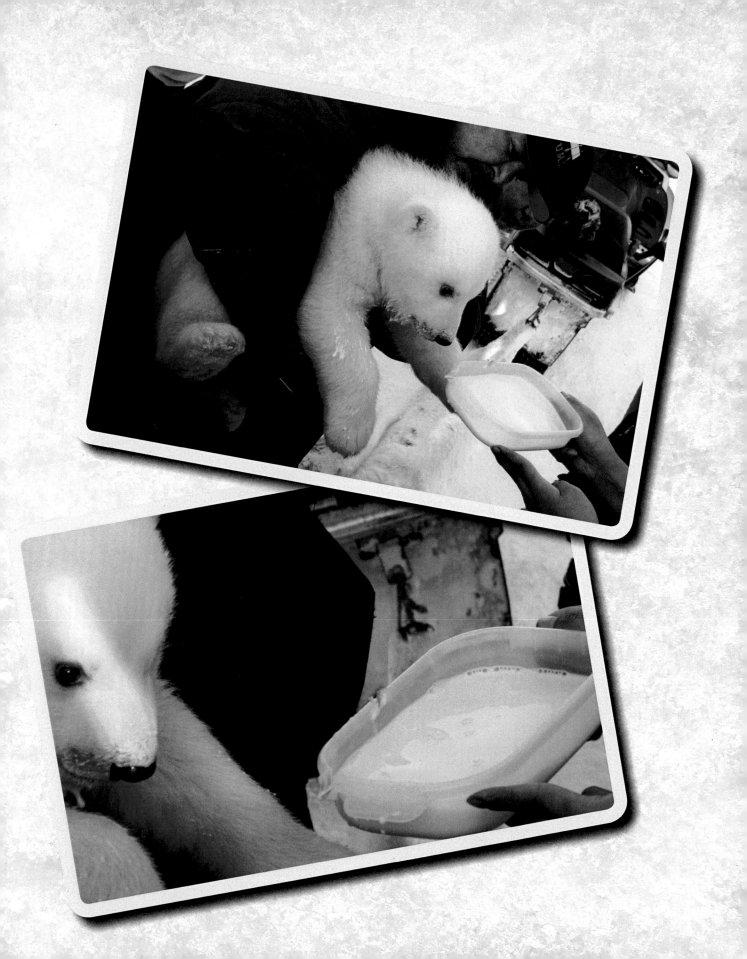

As the three-month-old bear rested in the police hall, villagers rushed to find a dog crate big enough to hold the fuzzy cub.

The villagers put Kali on a plane, and sent him to a wildlife vet and her team in North Slope Borough.

The vet checked Kali and said he was healthy enough for another plane ride to the Alaska Zoo.

It was just before midnight when Kali arrived at the zoo. Some polar bears huff or squeak when they are upset. Not Kali!

He was hungry. He eagerly drank from a bottle filled with fatty puppy formula and whipping cream.

Since the Alaska Zoo already had two adult polar bears, this would just be a foster home until a permanent home could be found for him.

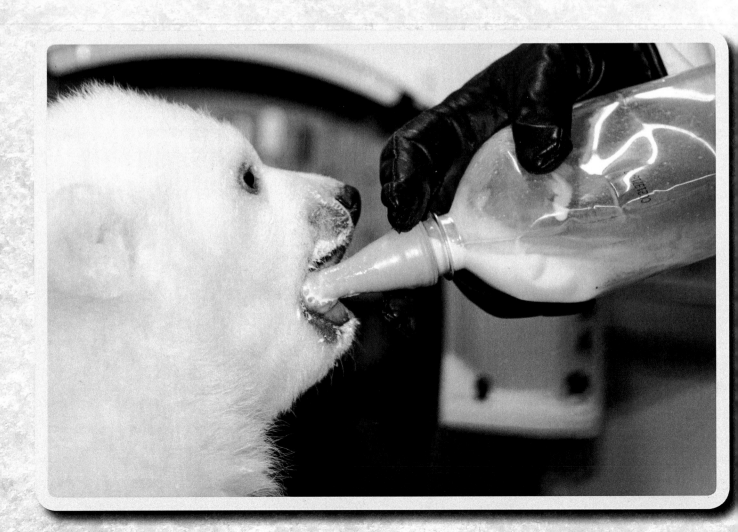

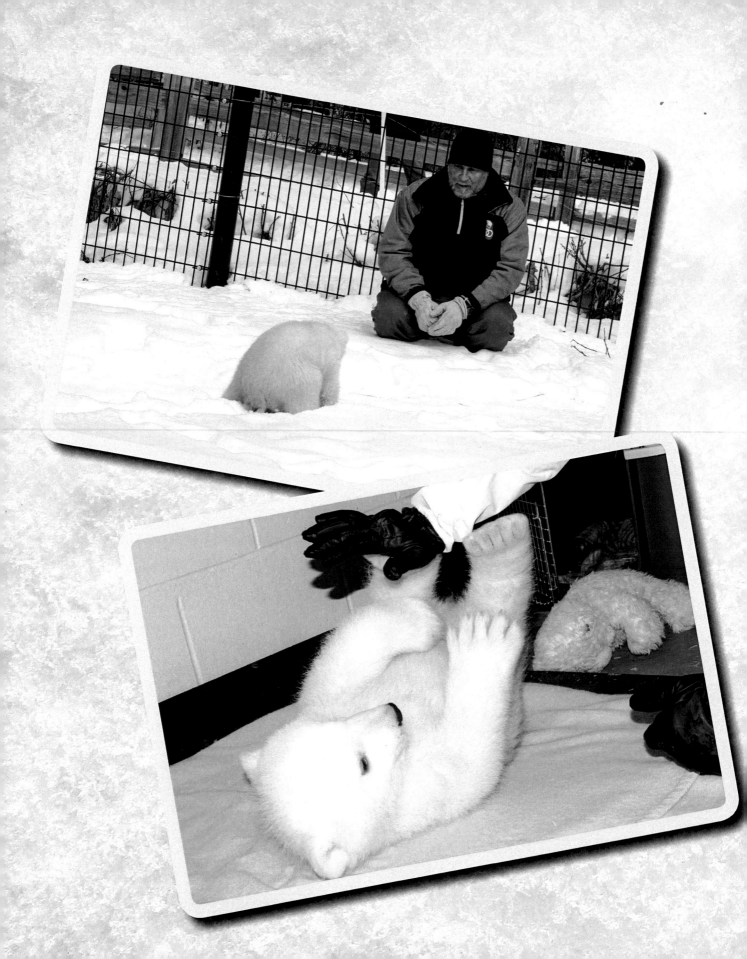

For the next three months, the playful young cub romped in his snowy habitat with the keepers.

In time, Kali began to eat solid food, like salmon and "polar bear nuggets," and to drink water from a metal bowl.

Kali also learned to swim—a very important skill for polar bears.

Kali practiced his hunting skills by playing with balls . . .

. . . toy dinosaurs . . .

. . . **and even a teddy bear!**

He climbed in and out of things . . .

. . . and then he took lots of naps.

Before long, it was time for Kali to go to another zoo. Although adult polar bears usually live alone, young bears need friends.

Luckily, for Kali, U.S. Fish and Wildlife officials found him a new home. At the Buffalo Zoo in New York, a girl cub named Luna was also in need of a friend.

To help prepare Kali for his journey, the Buffalo Zoo sent him one of Luna's blankets. The zookeepers hoped that Kali would get used to Luna's scent so he would recognize her when they met.

Soon it was time for Kali to take another plane ride. The Alaska Zoo bid farewell to Kali and wished him well in his new life with Luna.

During his first days at the Buffalo Zoo, Kali and Luna stayed in separate dens. They could hear and smell—but not see or touch—each other.

Although they were shy when they first met, they are now best of friends. They cuddle, play, and swim together.

Even though he is younger, Kali is now bigger than Luna. (Can you tell which polar bear is which?)

With zookeepers and vets caring for them, Kali and Luna will live happy and healthy lives.

Luna

Kali

For Creative Minds

This For Creative Minds educational section contains activities to engage children in learning while making it fun at the same time. The activities build on the underlying subjects introduced in the story. While older children may be able to do these activities on their own, we encourage adults to work with the young children in their lives. Even if the adults have long forgotten or never learned this information, they can still work through the activities and be experts in their children's eyes! Exposure to these concepts at a young age helps to build a strong foundation for easier comprehension later in life. This section may be photocopied or printed from our website by the owner of this book for educational, non-commercial uses. Cross-curricular teaching activities for use at home or in the classroom, interactive quizzes, and more are available online. Go to www.ArbordalePublishing.com and click on the book's cover to explore all the links.

Adapted for Life in the Arctic

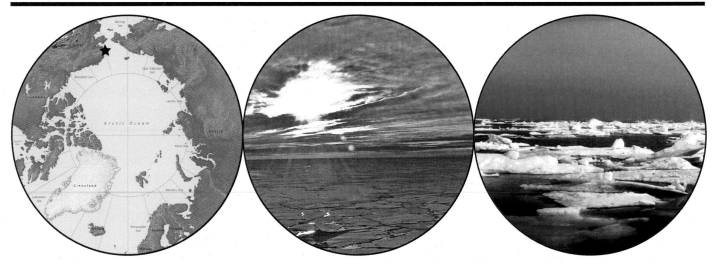

Polar bears live in the cold Arctic in the northernmost part of the Earth. The Arctic includes the Arctic Ocean and the land around it. Some of the Arctic Ocean is frozen sea ice. Some sea ice stays frozen all year long—even in the summer. Other sea ice freezes in the winter but then thaws in the summer.

During the winter, the Arctic is tilted away from the sun so there is little light or heat. Winter is cold and dark in the Arctic. During the summer, the Arctic is tilted toward the sun and it rarely gets dark. The weather might be warm, but it doesn't get hot.

Plants and animals, including humans, that live in the Arctic have adapted to the cold weather, the dark winters, and the light summers. Most of polar bears' lives are spent on and around sea ice and snow. Their bodies are designed to keep them warm on land and while swimming in the icy water.

Even though it is cold and dark, winter is a good time for polar bears to eat their favorite prey, seals. Seals live in the ocean, but breathe oxygen from the air. Seals poke breathing holes in the ice so they can get air. Polar bears hunt near these breathing holes and grab a seal when it comes up to breathe. When the ice melts the seals don't need breathing holes, and it's harder for the polar bears to find and catch their prey.

Polar bears do not live in dens except when female polar bears give birth. If the weather is unusually cold, polar bears might dig a temporary shelter in the side of a snowdrift. Otherwise, the polar bears roam for hundreds of miles to find food.

Polar bears have black skin under their fur to trap warmth and hold onto heat.

They have two layers of fur. The thick underfur is like a blanket—it insulates the bears to keep them warm. The outer layer of fur contains long guard hairs that are clear and hollow like straws. These hairs act like a wet suit to keep the underfur warm and dry. Polar bears can easily shake off water, snow, and ice.

We see white or cream-colored fur because of the way the sun reflects off the hollow hairs. The white-looking fur helps the bears blend (camouflage) into the snow and ice.

Polar bears shed and replace their fur (molt) every year during May or June when it is relatively warm.

Like other types of meat eaters, polar bears have sharp teeth to grab prey and tear meat.

Polar bear paws can be up to 12 inches (30 cm) wide. The wide paws act like snowshoes by spreading the bears' weight over the snow. The front paws are round in shape and the back paws are long. Each paw has five toes with claws that are used to grab prey and to run through the snow or on the ice. Pads on the bottom of the paws help prevent the bears from slipping on the ice. Hair grows between the pads and toes to prevent slipping and to keep the paws warm.

Polar bears swim for long distances. They have an extra, clear eyelid so they can see underwater with their eyes closed! When swimming, their ears lie flat and their nostrils close so water doesn't get in.

Polar Bear Math

It is pretty cute seeing photographs of Kali as a cub with zookeepers. But when Kali is fully grown, he will be too big to play with humans. Even though Kali is growing up around people in zoos, he is not a pet. He has instincts that could be dangerous to humans around him as he gets older and bigger.

Use measuring tools (a scale and a yardstick or tape measure) to compare the size of polar bears to things around you. What are some things that are similar in weight, length, or height? How do YOU measure up to a full-grown polar bear?

When born, polar bear cubs weigh 1 to 1.5 pounds (less than a kilogram). The cubs are around 12 inches or one foot long (30 cm). Males are larger than females, even at birth!

By the time the mother and cubs leave the maternity den, the cubs may weigh up to 33 pounds (15 kilograms). When Kali was found and taken to the Alaska Zoo, he weighed 18 pounds (8 kilograms). Zookeepers estimate that he was three months old.

Males (boars) are considered fully grown when they are 10 to 11 years old. Adult boars weigh anywhere between 770 and 1400 pounds (350 to 650 kilograms). They are 6.5 to almost 10 feet long (2 to 3 meters) and stand 5.3 feet (1.6 meters) at the shoulders.

Female polar bears (sows) are considered adults and start having young when they are five or six years old. Sows weigh between 300 and 550 pounds (150 to 250 kilograms) and can weigh twice as much when they are pregnant. The extra weight from pregnancy is not the cubs, but is extra fat that the females store to get through the winter. Once they enter the maternity den in the fall, they don't come out until spring. That's a long time to go between meals! Adult females are 5 to 8 feet (1.5 to 2.4 meters) long.

Image scale height of male polar bear:
child = 4 feet (1.2 meters)
adult woman = 5.5 feet (1.7 meters)
shoulder height = 5.3 feet (1.6 meters)
length/height = 10 feet (3 meters)

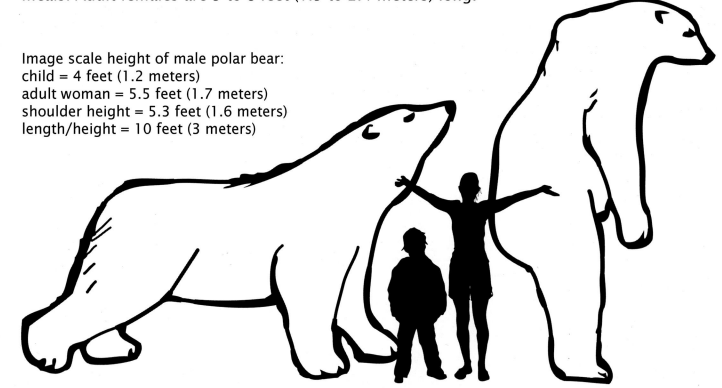

Polar Bear Life Cycle

Adult polar bears usually live alone. Polar bears gather together in feeding and breeding areas in April and May. Male polar bears will fight for the females.

Pregnant females will dig maternity dens between late August and the middle of October. They will not eat again until they leave the den with their cubs in the spring.

A polar bear mother usually gives birth to twins, but can also have just one cub or triplets. Cubs are born between November and January. When born, the cubs' fur is very thin so they snuggle up next to their mother to stay warm. Cubs don't open their eyes until they are about a month old.

The cubs spend the first few months of their lives nursing from their mother. They begin to walk when they are around two months old.

Mother and cubs leave the den in late March or early April. They will stay near the den for 1½ to 2 weeks before heading to the sea ice to get food. The cubs eat their first solid food when they are three or four months old.

Cubs learn to hunt by watching their mother. They can usually catch a seal or other food when they are a year old. Cubs stay with their mothers until they are 2 to 2½ years old. Then they will strike out on their own.

Scientists estimate that male polar bears in the wild live 15 to 18 years and females may live into their twenties.

Most of the images in this book were taken by John Gomes, the photographer at the Alaska Zoo. We would also like to thank the following people for sharing photographs with us that helped tell Kali's complete story:
In the story:
- Polar Bear Dens: Craig Perham, U.S. Fish and Wildlife Service
- Point Lay / Kali Village: Devin and Colby Way
- Arriving at Anchorage Airport: Charles Hamilton, U.S. Fish and Wildlife Service
- Luna and Kali playing: Kelly Ann Brown, Buffalo Zoo

Thanks to the following photographers for the use of their public domain photos that were used in the For Creative Minds section:
- Sun over arctic: Jonathan Wynn, U.S. Geological Survey
- Sea ice: Arctic National Wildlife Refuge-U.S. Fish and Wildlife Service
- Den opening: U.S. Geological Survey & U.S. Fish and Wildlife Service
- Hairless cub: Skandinavisk Dyrepark Zoo, Denmark
- Mother and cubs: Mike Lockhart, U.S. Geological Survey
- Two cubs: U.S. Fish and Wildlife
- Adult: Steven Amstrup, U.S. Fish and Wildlife

In appreciation and awe of teachers everywhere, especially those in the great state of Maryland.—JKC

Thank you to the following people who generously offered information and details for this book: The Alaska Zoo's Executive Director Patrick Lampi; Curator Shannon Jensen; and Keepers Lisa Ratner, Beth Fogleson, Jen Orr, Christin Groth, and Thomas Smith. Dr. Raphaela Stimmerlmayer of the North Slope Borough Department of Wildlife Management. Craig Perham and Charles Hamilton of U.S. Fish and Wildlife Service. Devin Michel Way of Point Lay.

In appreciation for their generous assistance, the author is donating a portion of the royalties from this book to the Alaska Zoo.

Library of Congress Cataloging-in-Publication Data

Curtis, Jennifer Keats, author.
 Kali's story : an orphaned polar bear rescue / by Jennifer Keats Curtis ; photography by John Gomes.
     pages cm
  Audience: 4-8.
 Audience: Grade K to 3.
 ISBN 978-1-62855-208-9 (english hardcover) -- ISBN 978-1-62855-217-1 (english pbk.) -- ISBN 978-1-62855-235-5 (english downloadable ebook) -- ISBN 978-1-62855-253-9 (english interactive ebook) -- ISBN 978-1-62855-226-3 (spanish pbk.) -- ISBN 978-1-62855-244-7 (spanish downloadable ebook) -- ISBN 978-1-62855-262-1 (spanish interactive ebook)
 1. Polar bear--Infancy--Juvenile literature. 2. Zoo animals--Infancy--Juvenile literature. 3. Animal rescue--Juvenile literature. I. Gomes, John (John G.), illustrator. II. Title.
 QL737.C27
 599.786--dc23
                    2013039470

key phrases for educators: Polar bear adaptations, Arctic, helping animals, zoos, life cycles

Title in Spanish: La historia de Kali: El rescate de un oso polar huérfano

Text Copyright 2014 © by Jennifer Keats Curtis

The "For Creative Minds" educational section may be copied by the owner for personal use or by educators using copies in classroom settings.

Manufactured in the USA
This product conforms to CPSIA 2008

Arbordale Publishing
formerly Sylvan Dell Publishing
Mt. Pleasant, SC 29464
www.ArbordalePublishing.com